Mucky Garden

Heather Finton

published 2017 by Northern
Undercurrents

ISBN 978-0-9958247-3-7

cover artwork by Danielle Pfeifer

Unexpected jewels,
this handful of companions
who call forth my authentic walk,
open-mouthed with pleasure.

I am honoured by your presence
in our journey together.

We were talking about all the weeds, that way of looking at a garden and being overwhelmed by all the green shoots poking through in unplanned places. The way a gardener can drive herself crazy with visions of how it could be, trying to create conditions for perfection or even just the constant pressure of noticing what could be better. Wanting everyone to be happy, even for an hour. Wanting to get rid of the weeds. Wanting a garden with no muck.

And how much gets missed in that stance, how the gardener loses out on the scents of what is here, the feel of mud between her toes, the beauty of long-awaited flowers, the unexpected native blossoms we call weeds.

A sweet freedom of enjoying rather than controlling or feeling responsible. A deep acceptance that a gardener does very little to nurture birth, that seeds and earth and air and warmth and water all move together in unseen ways, that life is creating itself all around us.

A profound relaxation into tending uncertainly, watering the tulips and letting the chickweed provide a little green along the border for a while, watching to see what is emerging. A deep trust in the transformative power of compost and decay.

A grin in the sunshine.

Portals for joy,
these shadows on my path
look like rocks,
tall boulders in way of the sun.

Except my new eyes
are learning to see
how the sunlight is bright
around the edges of these dark
encounters.

The scientists say
that nothing is solid;
I am starting to practice leaning,
pushing my attention
to the cold dark I want to walk around,
changing my contours
to let rock touch me,
its cold impossibility
warmed by my gut;
finding a new viscosity
as I move through what is here.

Raw onions on abraded skin,
wet glistening flesh,
the labia of listening

hot and quivering
and ready to bolt

to run and hide

except for love's command
to breathe

to welcome in

moist messy life

wrinkles and decay
with sweet juice

bright light of perception
as spotlight severe
and soft internal lamp
all at once;

don't run for cover.

Last night's moon
seemed broad enough
to carry my silent howl;
she stayed cold in the sky
but there was room
to offer my irritation,
let all my misalignment
and rough slivers of pains
fuel their own flight
to her orb.

And ego noticed
her reflective power,
how the moon could shine
my anger back into the talons
of a hungry owl,
into the rebellious heart
of a running mouse,
fuelling the wild voice
of a wolf calling for comfort.

An artist
in love with a blind man,
she paints extravagant beauty
rich with detail
she can only describe.

A musician
in love with a deaf-mute,
he plays new melodies
borne of love and tragic wealth
and she can only feel
the rhythm of his skin.

A dancer
in love with a paraplegic,
he watches her undulations,
feels the brush of her silk
like the exquisite promise of yesterday.

These are true stories of love,
the way it melts like honey
between two rocks unmoving,
the way its essence
is a teardrop,
its salty taste.

Like whales lost in the ocean,
our soundings ruptured by the noise
of all this industry,
it is hard to trust
in deep currents.

We groan our laments
and feel muffled in the waves of other sound,
amplifying our isolation.

Our moans are music.
The ocean is alive and carries our vibration.

If we keep strength
to howl our underwater truths,
surely our pod will find us,
one by one.

This grimace
is the face of me working
to interpret all these crashes,
the way wind has torn up
our neighbourhood,
the slamming of open doors
by unseen forces,
the unkindness
where once kites were eased skywards.

My ears have been dulled
by too much exposure
to roaring.
I am straining to listen again
to the whisper
and realize
that without ears or trees
or other obstacles
the wind is silent.

Trust becomes a very watery place, a lack of certainty and a falling into floating. I would like to know what happens next; whether the rush of poems is meant to go further afield or just be gratefully received as a healing, whether the floating uncertain quality of my desire and my marriage will find tender expression, whether the inner and outer contours of our lives will shift dramatically or imperceptibly.

I feel like I have gifts for visioning, planning, setting intention, but that I am being asked to radically drop all of that. I don't fear the floating, the welcoming of deep uncertainty and groundlessness – but I do fear my own ignorance/lack of wisdom/potential lack of stewardship or honouring. I truly want to honour and craft this life to the best of my ability, and am genuinely at a loss to know how much "crafting" versus how much being a blank page is the deepest vocation.

I have an arising sense that trust requires a lot of emptying so the page is blank or nearly so, and a willingness to scribe if there is anything in that space. I feel like I am in a pool of breathing water, and the paper of my five-year-plans and intentions is floating soggily somewhere above me, beloved but useless.

If not for the warmth of the word "trust" I would feel deeply unsettled, but it seems like a breathing tube so that I can see all this unexpected colour and new life in the salty deep core of my experience.

Leaving aside the point about God,
and whether divinity travels
inside this body
or in star dust
or not at all ever
or only sometimes

there is no doubt
that more goes on
than my eyes and shuttered mind
can let me see.

And no doubt
points to truth
and an unclenching of my fist
for an open palm,
an uncertain but resolved
welcome.

All this looking
for a doorway
to a garden
where the scents waft freely

when I notice
how my feet have crushed
a few petals
to make room
for sitting.

Whether the day has me panicked
on a forced march in desert;
treading water in a pool of others' need
while they cling for buoyancy;
hopping at full tilt
like a wobbly rabbit,
tufts of fur on thorns
leaving a trail for the fox…

there is the gift of pause,
forgotten but waiting always.

A small anointing,
oil on cracked skin,
sandbar under water,
stillness for a timid nose
to catch the scent of pine.

Dear worm,
you may long for past crawling,
warm branch on your belly,
or mourn for the way
you used to have all those muscles
inching you forwards,
allowing you to munch contentedly

you might have moments
of longing for the wrapping,
containment in cool
with all that reforming

you may even think
that you have gone backwards,
a heavy slouch
of devolution

but that is impossible
and your wings are real.

Do you see
how this longing to be more
is just a doorway
into laughter?

Ironic but not bitter,
the cosmic joke
unfolds softly
in a heart so full of discontent
there is no room for more;
and then the need of more
becomes a spacious dark
of never enough;
and in that warm dark,
a chuckle of satiation,
the not-enough
of all that is.

I can feel lost in the plethora, the many layers of my own story and the stories of those around me. I am learning to bring attention to what is here – but there is a lot here, and a lot that needs attention, and in some ways the increased awareness and perception just bring more layers of distraction, need and inadequacy.

Instead of "just" being present to one layer, there are all these connections that call for attention and care and settling in. Some are very practical – heat and food and cleanliness. Some are emotional – marriage and friendships and motherhood. Some are transactional – customer service, marketing, staff management. Some are artistic, creative or spiritual – perceptions of the natural world, translations into words and images and stories, opportunities for interaction and service beyond the day-to-day, inner experiences of joy and fear and awe.

And the jumble of all these layers is what life is about – the slight melancholy of awareness that it will always be jumbled, the slight joy and gratitude for the same humble mess.

God lives in you,
I see it wrapped
in the rich cloak of all of your habits,
shining under all those gnarled roots
and brilliant colours.

Sometimes you bedazzle
and sometimes hunker down
and I am not asking you
to fix anything
or wear different shades
or poke at any tubers

but just to notice
how God lives in you

and maybe loosen your grip
on the cloak that protects you

and raise your gaze
to see the ways I carry my own

and how the light shines anyway.

The poetry of my own body
rocking slightly on this cushion
while sun rocks over the mountains

the words below words moving through

gold lighting the underbelly of clouds

green continuing to grow like it did all night,

undulations of dawning.

Futures dance in front of me with open hands
like children inviting play,

like drops of paint or wisps of cloud

without picking and choosing

other than to grin.

A shaft of light
making space in a clouded sky;
like blowing dust from a bucket,
or finding a cushion
on which to sit differently.

Embracing no purpose
with open hands
once tangled in skeins of possibility

empty hands
that love the feel of threads
but can lie stilled
for the touch of air.

A vocation of blankness
is not what I expected
after all that offering,
those many uplifted gifts.

Look at all the people I could be
when I grow up.

See all my sketches
for a future life;
some of these doodles
show real promise.

Not just on paper,
see what I have crafted;
all these precious stepping stones to love,
these baubles of creation
even more lovely
than fridge door art,
though possibly less praised.

And so this call to an empty room,
or just an empty mind,
seems severe,
a serenity that might not understand
how busy I have been
with all this worthwhile bustling.

And this broom I wield
to sweep even an empty room
is one I that I must wrestle from my grasp
by stroking my own hands,
inviting me to lay it down
and sit without purpose.

Uncertainty can be destructive, either by pushing us off balance to a place of irrevocable wounding, or by constricting movement through indecision and fear of the unknown.

Even as I feel this understanding (mild nausea, repressed sadness), I also know that uncertainty is the birthplace of awareness, of curiosity and alertness, of possibility, of connection without preconception.

It is the womb of courage, that heart willing to feel vulnerable and loved.

Give me the desperation
of a houseplant,
lifting my leaves
to strain against the glass
for winter's hiding light,
stretching my roots
ever deeper through parched soil
in hope of water.

Let this drama
unfold without theatrics,
persistent and unyielding,
quietly contained.

May every drop of water
be absorbed,
working its transformation
in a dance with air and earth,
creating conditions
for even meagre light
to sprout vibrancy.

Sometimes I wake in the night
with unexpected hunger
and I live in a place
where a walk to the food is easy.

But it is good
to lie with unexpected gifts
and ask them to unwrap themselves,
and hunger is the same.

And really this is a hunger
for other kinds of love and feeding;
my ears and belly
want movement
but the journey is not to the kitchen.

Conch shells and pagodas.
inukshuks and camels,
exotic wonders
in a world
with a song to sing,
a melody enhanced
by pine trees,
refrigerators,
and the intricate warmth
of a baseball glove.

You are less deaf
than you think;
let the wax melt
with the heat
of your longing to listen.

How do I write a poem
about my need to choose
a decadent vacation?

Wanting time away to honour the goddess,
knowing that really means
time with friends I barely know.

Wanting seclusion with my husband,
warm caverns and bright rooms
for joy entwined,
for love in all its wrinkles,
tastes of fusion.

Wanting time to introduce my sons
to the world, journeying as family,
opening new vistas
for their own delight
in shaping who they choose to be.

What is the form
of this porous wall
that makes choice feel inevitable?

Big rocks,
she said,
put the big rocks
first,
commit to the weight of them
and they way they take up space,
make room in the bottle
for the big rocks.

Then the sand will sift in,
the small flecks
of glass in progress,
the myriad shiftings,
less relevant and still precious;
there will be room for all of it.

Light bends softly around his tender years,
the shock of pain this summer
felt as ripples through our scene,
love rising up
in its uncertain form,
vulnerable.

Valiant but not shielded,
open to his own need for reassurance,
the young knight
gambols armourless
in green fields of loss,
open to raw discoveries.

Beauty forged by blows,
he stands ever taller
in hesitant willingness,
touched by fingertips of wind.

Firstborn

When you were very small,
the nestling in
was obvious;
snuggling was part of your every hour
except for that rare dark pause
to experience isolation
before your wailing
called me close again.

And always as you grew
I found strength
in my settling in
to holding my arms wider,
learning how to hug myself
briefly
and re-open my arms
to cast my net a little farther
as you ran to explore
and returned with your discoveries.

These days you feel my web
as an entanglement,
a snare of constriction,
and you would tear it down
to wander in pure freedom.

That day is coming.
the future when you
will take your blade
to cut my ties
and walk only connected
with strings of your own making.

But here some joy
from the spider-woman:

notice how my webs
are spun of silk,
how the love that makes them
strong and supple
also brings you warmth,
how you can walk freely and tall
as they stretch to hold your changing shape.

Notice that the blade you hone
doesn't need to be a sword;
prepare instead the finest scissors,
carry their finesse
and snip gently
like a craftsman
patiently creating beauty.

with input from Sam

Backpack II

You mock traditional stories
and I don't battle,
since part of what you know
is their untruths,
which you reject.

And I have tried
to keep you from untruth
so that your spirit
burns bright,
with less to sort out later.

And struggled with my longing
to send you out prepared,
a backpack of fuel and protections.

Watch for these perils:
too much certainty of mind,
a barriered strength of heart,
gluttony.

Wear these amulets of exposure:
curiosity,
vulnerability in caring,
generosity.

Nourish your journey with:
astonishment,
simple and repeated thanks,
deep joy in now.

Aware of my own fluctuations, the way life is carrying platters of joy and stress to my feast, the way I see there is no "other life" to craft but that this one brings heartache and beauty in daily measure and will continue to do so no matter the circumstances of the story.

Yes I can choose more healthy practices (more meditation, writing, yoga, lovemaking, mealtimes...) but not as an "if/then" construction, not as a "someday" scenario. Change happens through embracing, not anticipating. And change continues to wriggle onwards in every hour, dancing alongside my effort and exhaustion, stomping on my sandcastles and making new mud pies.

Naturally I want to invoke "good" change – an evolution of peace and abundant living – but I have no clue about which choices lead to richer planes of existence, and I suspect that the rich river flows through all of it if I just remember to sniff for its deep wet.

Poetry for a deaf man,
I have followed his lead
trailing bright words of love
like petals of vibration
unnoticed

thinking he would hear
my call
to turn and see the colour
in all this generous scattering

wishing for the day
when joy would fill his heart
at the sound of my beautiful gifts

thinking his ears were stoppered
and he could find the plugs

and now I am reaching out gently
hoping not to scare

to touch his back
and gesture as he turns.

I love you
just the way you are
and
I have a really helpful list
of about 120 choices
you could make
to enrich the quality of your experience
and mine too

but I will set it down
again and again

because there is room here
for love now.

You handed me
yet another ice cube
and as the heat of rejection
and the fire of protection
were rising to keep it away

my tender lips
shaped themselves to say thank you

and my heart made room
for your cold gift

and then my voice awoke
to speak of love,

an ice cube dropped in a hot tub,

and laughed at my fear of cold;

and the hot splash of our sloppy souls
in beautiful familiar bodies
touched as never before.

And this is the magic of being,
pleasure's way of pouncing
when we drop our shields of knowing,

arpeggios of recognition
trailing ripples of sensation
in a song played only one precious once
by devoted musicians

who grin while waiting
for next time.

In this family I see my own journey on the ocean of integration and how I am spluttering in the waves often, and sometimes floating on them with skill. And the more I learn, the more I see the beauty and skill and spiritual journeying that is so clear in my husband and sons. But so far my attempts to express this seem to be heard not as affirmation and encouragement but more as judgment or pointing to how they could be different. Which leads to "not good enough" and separation from life right now.

So I can see how keeping silent and just noticing, being grateful, being loving is a less harmful path… but. But. There is also fear that by seeking a "less harmful" path of silence I am also avoiding risk, protecting myself from the vulnerability of speaking about possibility and affirmation.

This feels like a thick fog of uncertainty, a place where ego does not want to let go and I can't tell which part she's gripping, silence or speech.

I do sense that "calling forth" is mostly about listening… there may be words required, but in listening more deeply there is room for others to hear themselves.

A

And because so much of this
is fishing for the flashing,
trying to catch
the darting scales of love
in a flicker of words
before release,
an explosion of colour and movement
fleeting and always near

... I will wrap your body
in the way of tropical beaches,
salty and sublime,
heat and cool immersion,

all this underwater splendour
accessible and unseen from the surface,
where we share our daily peace
and long to frolic more often.

And yes, grey clouds come to the beach,
and even underwater the light can be dim,
but the plentitude roils always,
myriad shapes dancing,
love in our gills
always.

I am willing to shuck
the husks of my dead protections,
thanking them for services rendered,
dropping them for fodder

but can't tell
with this blind touch
where the dead wrappings lie
and which of them are damp

which sweet kernels underneath
must dry still further
or be consumed soon

how much longer
the withering

where the need is
for the feeding

human, cow or earth

and whether it matters.

The fact of my misalignment
has caused pain,
the way I sense true north
but can't approximate
its containment,
a slouch of northeast
or southwest,
tight patterns
of strength and lassitude.

For a while
I believed
that spinning
would widen the axis
and make more room
for a balanced centre,
shifting my friendship
with gravity.

I believed in the bright funnel,
receptive to the stars,
a flexible collector
for watering seeds.

Now I feel the kinks,
the puddles of inevitable waste,
the way that north is always out of view.

I cry with the gnarled feet
of a dancer too long on her toes.

Yes, there is still grace
in this shuffle,
a lined and ragged beauty
in this cramped hobbling

but close your ears

if you don't like rage,
turn your eyes
to a different stage
while I lie prostrate
on this one,
a furious intermission.

Help me to eat
my own fear,
not to make it go away
but to savour the taste of it

help me to let anger
roll on my tongue,
feeling its caress
on the inside of my cheek,
feeling it light my belly,
chewed and swallowed.

As I eat my own hunger,
salivating
with a fear of endless want,
let my tongue be freed
from labels,
sensitive to real flavours

ingesting all that I need
to spin
a necessary cocoon.

I have glimmers of realizing that my longing for more exposure and genuine self-acceptance and generosity in the world is really about the qualitative experience of my beingness, moment-to-moment.

The brilliant flashes of light and synthesis are not products on offer for others but are ways of seeing the world through my own eyes. I do feel some disappointment and sadness connected with this realization, but not enough to deaden my intention to write; just enough to temper it with the understanding that there is no audience waiting for my words.

It is the quality of light shining through that wants to find its way into the world and can do that through me every moment that I am open to it.

It's not fair
that we live in just one room,
not fair
that we only get
these trillion cells
in this configuration

not fair
that our lovers
aren't limitless

not fair
that we can only eat
one mouthful at a time.

I know this railing
is silly
but it is also true

there is regret
living in my belly

and it's not fair

when life drips with diversity
and my doorway
is so tiny.

Thrive

I have lived too long with a broom,
reaching to sweep clouds of hubris
and keeping the view clear
if somewhat chastised.

Dark clouds of wanting
swirl underground
where my broom will not go.

Attentive to the dangers
in pride and longing
and grand vision,
my belly clenches tight
to keep them out.

A clean and sterile hearth
stays cold;
mine is willing
to make space for fuel,
let longing nestle next to pride,
let all these visions burn with pure intent,
igniting warmth.

Here in the mess
of smoke and ash
a bright heat glows.

The fact of a butterfly

Thanks Adrienne,
and Matthew for reminding,
and Mom for all the fluttering.

But mostly thanks
to the teacher who noticed the crazy dance,
the frantic non-linear waving,
tasting the air at different levels,
aimless to the eye.

Thanks for seeing the brilliant colour,
suspended in vortices
of its own making.

Thanks for the reality
that when it stopped
and was so still,
it was almost unseen in its calm
and I had much to learn about waiting
to watch it fly again.

I was writing a poem
about madness,
how perhaps there are brothers too
and not just sisters
who understand what it is
to find no solace
and still be held
by an empty ground
that is mildly benevolent.

And then a fly
alighted on my knee
with intense vanity,
rubbing its front legs
with purpose or distress
and wiping its head
as if to clear its thoughts
or just shake dust off.

And then its vigorous balancing,
back legs kicking its own wings,
extreme grooming,
antics of self-care
laughable to see
in preparation for flight.

Life has pushed me into many situations of humility and vulnerability that have required me to stand exposed and raw, willing to listen. What has been revealed is a graceful touching of light on my wrinkles, a shimmering quality that dances over tears and snotty Kleenexes and stiff-but-willing asanas.

It allows me to see beauty hiding under ordinary coffee mugs and hear beauty hiding in words that used to close my ears.

I am grateful for these few descending breaths, like the space in the middle of a whirlwind, a slight opening of perspective where words are less significant and sensation is like a touch of emptiness, the hole in a dandelion stem, a reminder of roots.

When I say God
I don't mean a magic wand
or waiting for Godot
or any kind of king or queen

nor a loan guarantee
or teddy bear
or transportative breath or death.

And when I gnash and wail
or feel betrayed
or wallow in the ferocity
of my distrust,
I don't expect a messianic wind
or traveller's towel.

Yea, when I crawl through
the dark small shadow
of my insignificant stature,
there is no comfort
as my belly scrapes ground.

Only the leaves
whisper their complex song of surrender,
meaningless and free,
reminding me of my unintelligible dreams,
carriages in the dark
where I travel unbeknownst.

And with no hope of knowing
or being known,
creation and destruction
blend in the rising,
entwine in the falling down.

Burn off the fog,
rub my heart raw
until it shines like bright metal,
peeling and pealing,
sounding truth.

Oh yes I'd pick joy
or pleasure
or ecstasy
but let it ring
even when all is lost
or the clamour isn't pretty.

Even as I hear
how pointlessness sounds,
how futile the making
and impossible the travelling
to another ear untouched

let me want to be struck,
yearn to make noise
when the blows come

offering these notes,
being offered.

You've gotta get the tone
just right
or there is pain,
either yours because they lash out
or, damn,
you've caused it again

that smack of incomprehension,
that aimless fog of words
like woodsmoke
drifting just out of reach
and smogging the view.

You'll never get the tone
just right,
there is no way
to implant all sensations of a word
into another body
and even this voice
changes in an instant.

There is no safe way to speak,

no joy in keeping silent.

I may not look like
a friend to old farts,
in this pretty home
with my dyed hair
and all these gadgets

but if you see me grin
alone in the morning,
you might guess at my conversation
with men who rode on camels
and had to shake sand from their hair

and felt the grit of it
even as they savoured figs

and laugh at me down the ages
so that I am invited
to let my heart dance

here in my own desert
with the same particulate flakes
hiding everywhere.

There are moments
when life is safe and warm
with space for light to dance
and yet we are surprised
by the glint and scrape
of a Brillo pad
on the tender heart,

a rough tenderness
that does its work
when we let it.

And here the role
is not to press and scrub
or imagine future shining

but simply lie exposed
to stay with the abrasion.

You could take some time

to watch your own blossoming;

this water you have siphoned

from the everyday field

has caused a slow swelling

and the bud is fragile in its breaking.

There's nothing you can do anymore;

water, seed, soil have danced

to bring you to this stretched state

where green is slowly ripped

and a thin line of colour revealed.

Action will cause harm,

urgency interfere with savouring.

Just take a little time to marvel,

to let the pain of change be felt,

to sit in awe at the slow scene

of your own birth,

tender and curious.

A loveliness of dawn, quiet encounter with the deep ineffable. Am living the story of my days with more recognition of how each next moment arising is its own story and lesson and tender fruit.

And how I can't keep them all, but rather move through my days tasting, savouring, and dropping seeds wrapped in half-eaten fruit; hopefully there is a composting process at work behind my sticky trail!

Birdsong is now stronger and I am relaxing into an awareness of all the ways love holds me. Star Trek talks about a "space-time continuum" to describe interconnection but I think there is a space-time-love connection that helps infuse both space and time with more elasticity and energy when we make room for it.

Instead of being fearful about how I will "make" it all happen today, how I will meet others' needs and please them, how I will find the energy to stay grounded and busy when part of me wants to curl up in a hole... I can just allow love and trust to enter in and carry me. This is clearly prescriptive writing but good medicine.

Each of these cells
is making choices
about its genes and proteins,
hormones and neurons
and all the other links
I cannot see

and so I must surrender
to the wisdom of this body,
become embrained throughout,
let the juices flow where they will,
let the light of prana dance

willing to offer up detritus
and all the ways of weakness

allowing all the billions
to flicker
without constriction.

Pouch

When all this listening
causes my head to whirl
and vivid colours bloom in my heart,
vertigo seizing my day

let me drip my light
into the soft pouch of belly,
the furry kangaroo womb
resting on ground
through a tripod of strong legs and tail.

Let me draw strength
from earth
knowing that these thighs can leap,
resting on my haunches.

Let me draw comfort
from the warm enfolding,
awareness nestled low,
growing and protected.

Let me stoke my own fire
with the slow patience
of a dreamer camping,
idle, intent,
hearing crackles.

This faint ringing
or kind of buzz,
mostly in my left ear
like a dog alert on one side

there is space to make room
for listening,
and time to hear it
with no other need

even though all those needs
are knocking on the glass

my terrarium is warm
and vital
and the source of any growth

and here there is space for
– please hear, there is time for –
this quiet bell.

I feel all these projects in my body, a clenching of attention, a sense of responsibility and caring and wanting to do a good job. I can recognize this tension and choose to not let it be fear-based (fear of poor results, fear of not pleasing others, etc) but rather feel it as creative tension, the joy of ushering in caring and creativity, love and passionate endeavour... welcoming the tension rather than trying to calm, sedate or deny it.

Choosing to interpret the signals my own body and life experience are sending my way, rather than just reacting to them. It feels like a more raw experience, allowing room for the tension rather than trying to "manage my anxiety" by getting rid of it.

In making room, I also access this deeper laughter, this deeper and quieter wave of peace that laughs at the tension and the smallness of the projects that trigger it... connecting me to awareness of earth projects like mountains and hurricanes and sunrises... and other human projects, billions of them... my own will continue to rise and fall like heartbeats.

Inane patter,
these frothings of questions
about cloud colours,
comparing pink to grey

inanity a doorway
to the empty

bile as a conduit
to the void,
sliding over the razor wire
of judgment

to land scathing and scarred
in a stark quiet.

We humans are so fragile,
thin webs of fibre
carrying stories
with so little truth,
dancing with shadows
that often take the lead,
deaf to the true music
of silence.

So easily spun,
wounded and wound up,
tight patterns of worn turning on the floor,
or nauseous unravelling,
spinning out of balance.

All these stories of minds unleashed,
some as aspiration
and many knocked off centre
by waves of untouched feelings
or bodies speaking tortured truths

somehow the silence
calls us to hold melody,
reach out arms,
connect in caring circles.

There is a version of me
where the voice runs cool
like a river familiar
with its own banks,
echoing off its own carved spaces.

Not this swamp seep
rising with aimless attention
to nurture and make muddy,
forcing travellers to slog
or circumvent.

Oh, there are tendrils here,
and creatures used to murky light,
and very few boundaries
 - an interesting muck.

Gratitude for thaw
and all the ways of melting
has warmed this wetland.

Yearning for current,
a memory of flow,
this water is trying
to go somewhere.

I've been reflecting on my own sense of being "stuck" in uncertainty, wanting to summon up more decisiveness and choice and confidence in crafting what remains of my life. And I can feel how this is tempered by ego/fearful beliefs, negative thoughts around how life does not give us what we choose; as well as wisdom and spacious understandings, that grasping at choice and personal power is insignificant and pointless against the divine flow of life and death.

I feel very mid-life in this, understanding that choices and effort are ultimately "pointless" or do not give us ground in a groundless reality... and understanding that choice-making is our creative practice, that we are human bodies and human beings who are defined by the choices we make, how we can't just avoid our own capacity to choose but need to live it out daily.

And the creative tension between making choices and letting life choose (finding a surrendered or passive stance) is an acute tension for me these days, trying to liberate my own choice-making without strengthening my desire to be in control or have certainty just for the sake of false security.

Sometimes I feel like just a cramp,
one hundred muscles frozen,
a ball of ice
trying to melt itself
from the inside out,
afraid.

Merciless in my judgment,
I see the layers of my constriction,
all the ungiving,
the thousand times per day
I can't even relax
to sit without effort,
muscles lifting me
in a useless defense against earth,
breathing as a
necessary afterthought
through bound passages.

And despair has a bitter taste
I know well;
I keep swallowing
until my lips soften
just enough
to sip at kindness.

Everything hurts
and I'm OK
and everything hurts
and they're OK
and everything hurts
and we're OK

and not just as a gripping
in my head,
a desperate plea for safety

but as a river
in my aching soul
and flowing in this body
where I sit
and everything hurts
and it's OK.

How odd
to have picked an art
so linked with the monkey brain,
the nimble achiever

rather than the splashing of paint
or mixing of fresh herbs

and how delicious
to splash unambitious ink
on this useless, miraculous page
that has travelled far
to lie under my fingers.

Today I remembered my joy in our summer hammock, the shimmering light bouncing off the shivering, trembling poplar leaves.

I accept and make room for this aspect of me, this airy, light, sensitive, green, unsettled and constantly in motion aspect of my true nature... noticing my own edges of judgment (wouldn't an oak tree be "better"? a quiet lake?) but also a deep acceptance, a sliver of joy in seeing my own beauty in this, in expanding my heart to carry the many leaves, the cluttery fluttering, the hovering attentiveness and responsiveness that flits from need to need, the way that light shines on all of it and through my own ambivalent leaves.

Like a string of prayer flags, I have this reverent and celebratory quality that emerges when I let the wind blow through me and accept my own inevitable dangling, the limitations of my own string or roots, my tiny precious life.

I love the fierce magenta skies,
or deep blues that bring tears
because their tones are so beautiful

but many mornings
are like this one,
the soft creep of
night into light,
variations on words
for white, hued
with yellow, peach, robin's-egg,
slow and subtle changes.

And so my art
is not about cans of paint
splashed in vibrant rooms

but just this quiet striving
to wrap fresh names
around the ordinary.

There are times when I know
that eight or ten creeks
mark the flow of this life,
each diverse stream
with its own gurgles or roaring
and me tending
all these waterways,
rivulets and rivers.

And so my mouth can gape
with no articulation,
no frame for all these
ways of being.

But here the invitation;
hear this open-mouthed silence
as we hover briefly
where the deep convergence
gathers all this water.

If I met her in person
she would raise one gentle finger
to quiet my turmoil
and tell me to do
what needs doing;

and see I am listening already.

I hear the wide expanse
of a voice from broad hips
inviting me to hush,
to settle back,
to drink deeply
at the start of a necessary journey,

to move now
before tomorrow,
and trust that the river
will quench all thirst.

with thanks to CPE

The angry banshee
howling in my ribs
makes hollow song
that I keep ignoring

but I fear her poison
and so she spins and wails
at the edge of my register

and I keep wincing
but don't know why,
blocking out a sound
I barely hear,
like white noise
only darker.

Sing, you crazy witch,
my ears are willing to float,
trolling my bloodstream
and following the echoes
as you beat on lonely walls.

Sing out your story,
distorted and true,
let me find you
not for battle
but a kind reckoning.

Breath as an entry point to felt experience, my guilt and its underlying sadness around personal limitation, the sort of existential sadness around not being "everything," experiencing life through differentiation and limitation and mortality, the deep sadness around "not enough" and the way we inevitably cause harm to ourselves and others.

And by feeling this sadness and the pattern of guilt and defensiveness that has protected me from the sadness… a deeper self-acceptance, more capacity to love me, to feel compassion surge through my unclenching muscles and thawing heart.

A willingness to let guilt and sadness be present but also to let them float away and make space for kindness, joy. Awareness that limitation provides a container, a lamp in which light can flicker and be warm.

That nausea,
the bile that comes
from seeing a leaf curled and dying,
life three quarters done,
or a spider's work in progress
near a rising broom;

that same dread
spills relentless
into fingers holding the remote,
mouths gaping at the fridge,
dazed shoppers buying dye.

We have few gloves
to handle these hawks,
few choices in their feeding,
so they scrabble
and gnaw unseen
while only rarely
is there husbandry
to feed and let fly
and welcome home.

I have a friend
in great pain
and many stories
of how it might have come to be

and how it might
be a doorway

and how there is constriction
in the love
trying to be shared

and sorrow unspoken

and how it is not that easy

and being with it is hard

and I started out
thinking of my friend
and here we are.

I am not looking for a life "out there" or different from all the many abundant choices I have here. What I want to do is make more room here for my own deep journey and for this activist energy of wanting to help with transformations other than my own.

And noticing how the two are linked, how much the "other" focus comes as a result of this inner work, not necessarily as a result of will and effort so much as aspiration, intention and willingness to receive.

With a dose of patience, but not complacency, and learning to know the difference.

So used to war,
to battles dividing,
the need to solve
and fix, erase
whatever ails

and now this voice
inviting me to dance,
to spin the yin and yang,
make space for my enemy,
embrace the pain
that lives here.

Peace must be like this,
a natural agitation,
a spin cycle blending,
a way of refusing to fight
and still dance with power.

There are women who know,
speaking their silence
like taking off a veil
and showing the silk underneath,
the right colour for now,
enhancing the room
until it is time for more revelation.

Of course they have sounds,
they speak their wisdom
like the splash of a stone down a well,
but between them
there is no need for noise,
a glance trading tales.

Preserve me
from my own seeking,

shelter my gaze
so my shutters are sprung wide
to catch the lights nearby,
to feel the supple threads
of my own weaving,
to throw down
my own embroidered offerings.

There are more skillful teachers
and I am not too proud
to beg for help

but have not found their ears

and so must listen
to the half-light inside,
the shadowed lamp.

For so long I feared
the spectre of my own darkness,
tiptoeing through my body,
rainjacket against the splash
of my own feelings

knowing a maze and a minotaur,
cautious turnings.

Now I am starting to wander
more bravely,
watching how shadows make beauty,
reminders
of the glow
I carry so gratefully.

Was looking for the pearl of my vitality, listening to belly, when I encountered an ancient, barnacled, mountainous sea hag, a deep and powerful encrusted matriarch planted like a fountain of solidity at the bottom of the sea.

A bright pearl rested on her tongue but it was almost a bauble compared to the dark majesty of her fearsome presence, shapeless like a lumpy oyster shell growing from the ocean floor.

Descending rows of women were circling this underwater mountain grandmother; a line of ancient mothers, then middle mothers; a circle of priestesses, witches and sages; and hundreds of sensuous mermaids at her base.

She groaned her amusement at my search, showing me all the layers of vitality, how it sometimes means the bright sinuous flash of scales but also resides in the slow wisdom of rock, and how it can be all of these at once.

She also taught the value of descent, of being touched by salt and wet and cold to find the bounty undersea, the value in seeing how the object of our search is such small treasure against the crashing powerful ageless flow of life.

What is the core inhibition?
She asked me
with the pure intent
of one who is willing to heal

and I can't quite trust
that there is an answer,

one significant lesion
ready for binding.

I have always felt
like a collection of small scratches
or decades
of short breaths

sand abrading caves

is there an exit

for standing in the wind

and why do I fear the exposure?

My metal spoon
can stab that brown sugar
to no avail,
chipping only minor flakes of sweet,
a light dusting
in the middle of exertion
and pointless effort.

Or it can slip under the lump,
accept its rocky burden,
lift it
to where it can be dropped
and instantly sweeten
my warm wet brew.

Like work in a steel mill,

loud and hot,

whirling vortices of activity

trudging relentless,

the need to scream

to be heard

and all that ear protection.

Interconnected,

these hives

all move the steel

continuous,

lumps of dirt

to molten,

measured hardness,

shipping forth.

Complex and simple both,

improving and degrading;

shortages and plenty

have their pressures,

prana in real life.

Left-handed

Forced to slow
like aging overnight
and shaping each letter with care

I learn about slanting backwards
and brand new shapes
and how this voice
is familiar and less urgent

fearful of limitation
but willing to play.

I read my wobbling script
while my right hand hovers
as if it could help
or take over
and hear unspoken judgment
yet I persist
in this crude listening.

I am experiencing some release in noticing, separating from the storyline, breathing in the shame/sadness/guilt, breathing out forgiveness for myself and the billions of others who also make mistakes and feel shame.
Realize the inevitability of shame, the way that we teach each other so many stories of warning in an act of love, so many stories of how humans need to make good choices and the tragedies when they don't anticipate their results… these warnings are part of our collective heritage, our ways of protecting our children.

We also need tools for teaching about resilience instead of blame, laughter in the midst of mistakes, acceptence of how we will not choose wisely all the time.

Our suffering (health, relationships, money etc) is linked to our choices, and we have choice in the ways we can aspire or hope to make change, but we did not design the breadth of our experience; we can't hold ourselves responsible for existential suffering; it is inevitable and I need to lessen my grip on the subtle blaming of myself and others when I am aware of how we suffer.

Regardless of how we got here, to a present moment of suffering, a present moment of shame or pain, the liberation is kindness to the moment itself, without trying to trace back the path that got us here or anticipate a pathway out.

So many hurts and "could be betters"… sometimes it feels like a cop-out to fall into love and gratitude, but sometimes it is the only way to break the inertia and overwhelm. I am grateful for this mysterious body, this multi-layered mind, this generous and constricted heart, my wonderful-and-messed-up-and-blessed husband, my beautiful-and-unknown-and-familiar children, this fabulous planet and all the ways life is teeming all around.

If the choice is to savour or reject, I choose savouring.

Thank you,

bright one,

for dancing on this page

and in my days

like a shaft of sunlight

carried on fresh wind,

the gift of your friendship

surprising

in a life lived largely on this couch,

gazing at the long view.

The crackle of your fire

is welcome song;

how astonishing

to weave new melodies.

Aaah…

the underscore of poems,
like a space for melody
to drizzle
art and drivel,
the soup where bliss and blah
simmer intermingled,
the scent
before the tasting.

All this sublime talk,
meditation and states of being...

another way to say
go camping
without all the gear,
wake each morning and light the fire
inside you,
watch it for a while
without thinking or moving much,
see if it warms you.

Go fishing
through the remnants of your dreams,
use a gentle net or pole,
enjoy the pointless waiting,
the empty-handed days;
describe any beauties
and release them.

Breathe in,
your own smoke and fresh air mingled;
breathe out the same stuff,
slightly changed
by its journey
through your lungs.

The teachers laugh
at our puzzled frowns
because they are happy
we're on track.

So when they say breath,
they mean a metaphor
for prana,
or the golden light
or sometimes it is dark velvet
and it ebbs and flows

except that it is not just metaphor
and so they really mean
the air you actually
pull through your nose,

and then they don't,
and they they do, again,

and you might as well
grin with them.

What if today
I set down the list
and let my skin
take charge?

What would my skin
choose right now?

Probably water,
inside and out,
and that could take a while,
a treasure of decadent moments.

It loves to stretch,
to flex and thrust,
plumping itself full of light
in all directions

and would seek
to be oiled
and offer oiling
to intimate friends

and once soothed,
make softened greetings
to strangers.

Am amazed by the way my soul calls me early
each morning, inviting me to come and dance.
And somewhat saddened by the way I hold
worry in my body – literally clenching shoulders
and belly and thighs – and how many breaths
to begin the relaxation, even when I am aware
of the holding.
Sadness only for my limitation, whatever
prevents me from diving in to a warm pool of
confidence, love and comfort.

More like standing, shivering but somewhat
brave, at the top of a slide, knowing where
water is.

It is good

to get your work done

before you play

and you will never get your work done

and you need to play

and I know how this goes

how mid-life can feel

like there is barely a memory

of what play can be

how we find moisture

in a bottle

for daily application

to disguise dryness

but there is water;

follow your roots,

pretend to play

with genuine intent

and splashing will find you.

Lighten up,

let your light twinkle
in your cells
as if you'd forgotten
how to find the switch
and stumbled on it in the dark.

Flip it,
find the dazzle
in your day to day,
drop the armload of shoulds

… no, really,
drop it.

Or if you're afraid of crashing noises,
lay it gently on the ground
and step back
just one pace
and see what happens to your stance.

Notice how sometimes
there's a smile under your ribs
that just needs a little freedom.

Like a lonely stadium
waiting for action,
transform your space
by releasing light
waiting in your walls.